THE LITTLE BOOK OF FISHING TIPS

D0717019

MICK DEVENISH

THE LITTLE BOOK OF
FISHING
TIPS

MICK DEVENISH

Absolute Press

First published in Great Britain in 2007 by
Absolute Press
Scarborough House, 29 James Street West
Bath BA1 2BT, England
Phone 44 (0) 1225 316013 **Fax** 44 (0) 1225 445836
E-mail info@absolutepress.co.uk
Web www.absolutepress.co.uk

A catalogue record of this book is available
from the British Library

ISBN 13: 9781904573661

Printed and bound in Italy by Legoprint

'When the wind is East,
The fish bite least,
When the wind is West,
The fish bite best'

Anon.

Local knowledge

of any fishing situation

is invaluable

so always talk to other anglers and ask questions about the best times, conditions and methods for fishing. Most anglers are friendly and nowhere near as competitive as folklore would suggest.

No matter how expensive your fishing tackle

the only bits the fish will see are the hook and bait

so take time to make sure they are presented properly and in a manner that looks natural to the fish and doesn't discourage them from biting.

When approaching the river or lake

always keep a low profile.

The fish will see you silhouetted against the pale sky long before you see them in the darker water. Camouflage clothing is also very useful to avoid being seen.

Tread carefully

and don't make a lot of noise by the waterside.

Fish use their whole body to
detect
vibrations so, like all wild

creatures, will be aware of your presence before you are aware of them.

Tackle Bag Essentials No.1: Fingerless neoprene gloves

are one item of clothing that can make a big difference to your fishing session on a cold day.

When choosing where to fish, look for features

like overhanging branches and submerged obstacles such as sunken trees

which will attract fish

looking for cover against predators. Fish in the sea will also colonise a new wreck very quickly in their effort to find safety.

Plumb the depths of your local water to determine what depth you should fish at

and make notes in the low-water conditions of summer about features which will be invisible to you in winter. Fish will frequently shoal up in deep holes in winter and knowing the location of these can be invaluable.

When stalking a stream or river

always cast upstream, against the current.

Fish will generally lie head on into the current to minimise the effort needed to hold their position so you will be approaching them from behind.

Always buy whatever fishing license or permit is required

for the situation and observe any bye-laws. How can you expect to relax and enjoy yourself if you are breaking the law?

Handling Rule No.1:

When handling your fish

get your hands wet and use a damp towel.

This is safer for you and is also better for the fish if you intend to return it to the water.

Keep notes of your fishing sessions for future reference and take a camera to

record your catch. If no one is available to

photograph you with your fish lay it down next to your rod to give scale.

Buy a hook file and use it regularly.

Regardless of the type of fishing you are doing a blunt hook will drastically reduce your chances of a positive hook-up.

Line is fairly cheap and damage to it can often not be seen. To avoid losing the catch of your life **it is always worth discarding 3–4 yards of line** off the reel **after every fishing trip** and starting your next session with a new length.

If you are **coarse fishing** and intend to catch and release your fish then **use barbless hooks every time.** A skillfully played fish kept on a tight line is just as safe on a barbless hook.

15

If you must use

a keep net it must now be of a knotless construction

to avoid damaging the fish. It is best, however, to avoid using one altogether.

Very small hooks are difficult to tie on, so **try buying packs of pre-tied hooks to nylon** which can easily be added to the cast.

You don't need to know how to tie many knots to be an angler but **knots are essential to good fishing** so learn a few and practise tying them well.

When tying knots in nylon monofilament

wet the knot with saliva before pulling

it tight. The lubricating and cooling effect of this will make a stronger knot.

Nylon monofilament or braid?

Both have their uses but essentially mono has a lot of stretch and good rub resistance against trees and rocks, etc., but it is more than twice the diameter of braid. Braid has virtually no stretch which can put you in much better contact with your fish and give a more positive hook set, but it does fray on contact and will weaken quickly.

If catching lots of fish

is your main priority then

buy a pole

and learn how to use it. They are expensive but they allow you to fish a very small area with great accuracy.

Handling Rule No.2: Carry forceps and long-nosed pliers

and keep them near to hand. This will ensure you can always remove hooks with the minimum of fuss and risk to you and your fish.

Never discard old fishing line.

Take it home, chop it into small pieces and preferably burn it. This avoids it getting into landfill sites and potentially causing suffering to animals and birds.

A trip to the modern tackle shop can be a bewildering experience for the average pleasure angler but 'keep it simple' is generally the best advice. Over-complicated and fussy rigs can be more trouble than they are worth and a lot of

fancy tackle often seems designed **to catch more anglers than fish.**

An old fridge

is worth hanging onto

for storage of all types of bait.

Maggots will live for a week or more in a secure breathable container and most paste balts, though not as good as freshly mixed, can be frozen and re-used.

Worms are still one of the best baits to use for all types of fish and **chopped up** they **produce an irresistible smell trail.** They are best kept in a breathable box filled with moss and put in a cool place for a few days before use. This toughens them up and they will stay on the hook for a lot longer.

Grazing fish such as tench or bream can often be **located by** observing the **small clouds of bubbles** which are released as the fish search the lake bed.

Don't underestimate **carp:**
they have great power so tackle needs
to reflect their strength.

Fish the surface and the margins in summer for the best results.

28

Target pike in the winter

when they are fully recovered from spawning and in peak condition and hungry. Try fishing a diving plug or spinner to imitate a wounded bait fish. Move location every 20 minutes or so to find the fish and also stay warmer yourself.

Perch can be caught with plugs and spinners but they **absolutely love worms.** Smaller perch will shoal up but the bigger specimens tend to be lone hunters.

A hat and glasses are essential for fly or lure fishing

to protect the face and eyes from flying hooks when casting.

Handling Rule No.3:

When catching and releasing any reasonably sized **freshwater species** hold the fish upright in the water by the tail end and rock it backwards and forwards to work the gills for a few moments, it will swim safely away when it is ready to go. Generally speaking, the larger the fish the longer it will take to recover.

When the sun is out

use polarised sunglasses.
They will cut through the surface reflection and glare allowing you to see right into the water and saving you a possible headache too.

If you are fishing alone tell someone where you are going and an expected time of return. Better to be safe than sorry.

Fishing in the rain can often be well worth the effort but **never fish** in a storm **with the risk of lightning** or near overhead power cables. It is hard to imagine a better conductor than 10 feet of carbon-fibre fishing rod.

When loading line onto a fixed spool reel

the line should come off the end of the line spool in the same direction as the rotation of the bale arm on the reel to avoid pre-twisting of the new line.

Tackle Bag Essentials No.2: A head torch can be crucial.

It enables you to see what's happening whilst keeping both hands free to catch that record-breaking fish which you hooked after dusk.

Always **check the drag setting** on your reel **before starting to fish** and set it so that you can just pull line off the reel by hand. Too tight and a striking fish could break the line, too loose and you will not set the hook.

A sea sickness tablet taken before leaving port

in the morning should guarantee that your day on the sea is not spoiled by unexpectedly rough conditions. Your companions will certainly not thank you for wanting to go back before the trip is over.

For offshore sea fishing, **rigs and traces are best tied up** at home **before you get on board** a pitching charter boat in the sea. They will be stronger and you will be safer.

Sea bass are one of the best fish to eat and **can often be caught with a spinner in the breaking surf** on a beach, but remember that it is illegal to take them under 36cm long.

Don't be frightened of the Pike if you catch one.

Although it is a fearsome predator and has a mouth full of sharp teeth **it can be lifted easily** by inserting the fingers into the cleft under the chin and holding around the tail.

After a sea fishing trip, rinse your reel

in warm clean water. Removing the corrosive salt will add years to the life of this expensive piece of tackle.

When tying a hackled fly

onto your leader, first push the hook eye through a leaf. This will hold back and protect the hackle and **avoid the fibres becoming mixed** in with your knot. The leaf can then be torn off easily and the hackle will remain undisturbed.

Buy good

line scissors or clippers and attach them to your jacket with a retractable 'zinger'. This way, they will always be

available when you need them (usually when your hands are already full with a trace or rig that you have just tied up).

To weigh a specimen fish

always place it into a bag first then deduct the weight of the bag from the total. Never hang a fish from the hook of a balance by the mouth or gill cover.

The art of casting a fly

can only be learned with practice but keeping the wrist on your casting arm rigid and in line with the forearm is essential. Keeping the rod tip working between 10 o'clock and 2 o'clock will also help greatly.

Tackle Bag Essentials No.3: sun block

Always keep **sun block** in your tackle bag and remember to use it. UV rays reflected off water are no different to a mirror and you can burn badly before realising it.

Protect your fly lines from drying and cracking

by cleaning and re-plasticizing regularly, once every season as a minimum. This is quick and easy to do and has the added bonus of helping your casting.

When sea fishing over rocky ground for species such as wrasse, **use old nuts and bolts for weights** and attach them to the cast with a 'rotten bottom' length of weaker-knotted nylon. Much cheaper than lead.

For the beach angler, the best time to start fishing

is often a couple of hours before high tide. The movement of rising tide on coastal water will unearth the food species such as shrimps that attract fish in to feed.

Mick Devenish

Mick Devenish wasted much of the first fifty years of his angling life being a successful businessman and mortgage payer. From childhood messing in streams and ponds to fly fishing for trout, his piscatorial horizons gradually expanded to include coarse and sea fishing throughout the UK along with regular expeditions to the remote jungle rivers of the Amazon basin in search of exotic and predatory species. He has also fished extensively in India, Africa and Central America. At home in the south-west of England he keeps koi carp in his garden pond and stocks and runs a small trout lake with friends.

THE LITTLE BOOK OF
BARBECUE
TIPS

ANDREW LANGLEY

THE LITTLE BOOK OF
BEER
TIPS

ANDREW LANGLEY

THE LITTLE BOOK OF
HERB
TIPS

WILLIAM FORTT

THE LITTLE BOOK OF
POKER
TIPS

THE LITTLE BOOK OF
GARDENING
TIPS

WILLIAM FORTT

THE LITTLE BOOK OF
CHEFS'
TIPS

RICHARD MAGGS

THE LITTLE BOOK OF
SPICE
TIPS

ANDREW LANGLEY

THE LITTLE BOOK OF
GOLF
TIPS

PETER FRENCH

THE LITTLE BOOK OF
TIPS
SERIES

THE LITTLE BOOK OF
CHEESE
TIPS
ANDREW LANGLEY

THE LITTLE BOOK OF
WINE
TIPS
ANDREW LANGLEY

THE LITTLE BOOK OF
AGA
TIPS²
RICHARD MAGGS

THE LITTLE BOOK OF
COFFEE
TIPS
ANDREW LANGLEY

THE LITTLE BOOK OF
TEA
TIPS
ANDREW LANGLEY

THE LITTLE BOOK OF
AGA
TIPS³
RICHARD MAGGS

THE LITTLE BOOK OF
AGA
TIPS
RICHARD MAGGS

THE LITTLE BOOK OF
CHRISTMAS
AGA
TIPS
RICHARD MAGGS

THE LITTLE BOOK OF
RAYBURN
TIPS
RICHARD MAGGS

THE LITTLE BOOK OF
BRIDGE TIPS

PETER FRENCH

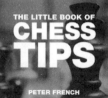

THE LITTLE BOOK OF
CHESS TIPS

PETER FRENCH

THE LITTLE BOOK OF
FISHING TIPS

MICHAEL DEVENISH

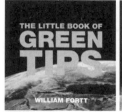

THE LITTLE BOOK OF
GREEN TIPS

WILLIAM FORTT

THE LITTLE BOOK OF
KITTEN TIPS

ANDREW LANGLEY

PAUL HARTLEY
THE LITTLE BOOK OF
MARMITE TIPS

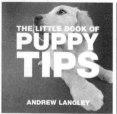

THE LITTLE BOOK OF
PUPPY TIPS

ANDREW LANGLEY

THE LITTLE BOOK OF
WHISKY TIPS

ANDREW LANGLEY

THE LITTLE BOOK OF
TRAVEL TIPS

MEGAN DEVENISH

Little Books of Tips from Absolute Press

Tea Tips
Wine Tips
Cheese Tips
Coffee Tips
Herb Tips
Gardening Tips
Barbecue Tips
Chefs' Tips
Spice Tips
Beer Tips
Poker Tips

Golf Tips
Aga Tips
Aga Tips 2
Aga Tips 3
Christmas Aga Tips
Rayburn Tips
Puppy Tips
Kitten Tips
Travel Tips
Fishing Tips
Marmite Tips

Forthcoming Titles:

Green Tips
Whisky Tips
Bridge Tips
Chess Tips

All titles: £2.99 / 112 pages